Contents

What to Do 2

An Amazing Find 4

A Bird-Like Fossil 6

A Huge Animal 8

Other Huge Birds 10

Big – Good or Not So Good? 12

What Next? 14

Something to Think About 16

Do You Need to Find an Answer? 18

Do You Want to Find Out More? 19

Word Help 20

Location Help 23

Index 24

What to Do

Choose a face

Remember the colour you have chosen.

When you see your face on the page, you are the LEADER.

The LEADER reads the text in the speech bubbles.

There are extra words and questions to help you on the teacher's whiteboard. The LEADER reads these aloud.

When you see this stop sign, the LEADER reads it aloud.

STOP
My predictions were right/wrong because . . .

You might need:

- to look at the WORD HELP on pages 20–22;
- to look at the LOCATION HELP on page 23;
- an atlas.

If you are the **LEADER**, follow these steps:

1 PREDICT

Think about what is on the page.

- Say to your group:

"I am looking at this page and I think it is going to be about…"

- Tell your group:

"Read the page to yourselves."

2 CLARIFY

Talk about words and their meaning.

- Say to your group:

"Are there any words you don't know?"

"Is there anything else on the page you didn't understand?"

- Talk about the words and their meanings with your group.
- Read the whiteboard.

- Ask your group to find the LET'S CHECK word in the WORD HELP on pages 20–22. Ask them to read the meaning of the word aloud.

3 ASK QUESTIONS

Talk about how to find out more.

- Say to your group:

"Who has a question about what we have read?"

- Question starters are: how…, why…, when…, where…, what…, who…
- Read the question on the whiteboard and talk about it with your group.

4 SUMMARISE

Think about who and what the story was mainly about.

When you get to pages 16–17, you can talk to a partner or write and draw on your own.

 or

An Amazing Find

Xu Xing (*Shoo Shing*) is a scientist in China. One day, he found a **fossil** of an enormous animal. It was an animal that had lived millions of years ago.

At first, Xu Xing and other scientists thought it was a fossil of a **Tyrannosaurus rex**. Then they found it was the fossil of a bird-like dinosaur.

They called the fossil Gigantoraptor.

I am looking at this page and I think it is going to be about… because…

Are there any words you don't know?

Who has a question about what we have read?

Let's check: fossil

Why do you think the scientists thought the fossil was of a Tyrannosaurus rex?

Xu Xing carefully uncovers a fossil.

This page was mainly about ___ fact ___ fact

STOP
My predictions were right/wrong because . . .

A Bird-Like Fossil

The Gigantoraptor had huge claws. It had no teeth, but it had a snapping beak. This was probably for tearing meat. It had a small head and a long neck, like an **ostrich**.

The scientists thought it could probably run very fast.

They also thought that it may have had feathers. In some ways, it may have been like birds in our world today.

I am looking at this page and I think it is going to be about... because...

Are there any words you don't know?

Let's check: model

Who has a question about what we have read?

Why do you think the scientists thought the Gigantoraptor could probably run fast?

Xu Xing stands next to the fossils and a **model** of Gigantoraptor. Its claws were like sharp **daggers**.

This page was mainly about... fact fact

STOP
My predictions were right/wrong because . . .

A Huge Animal

The scientists were surprised at how big the Gigantoraptor was. Other bird-like dinosaurs had been found, but they were much smaller than this giant!

The Gigantoraptor was twice as tall as a person. It was 35 times heavier than any **feathered** dinosaur that anyone knew about.

The Gigantoraptor was quite young when it died. It could have grown even bigger!

I am looking at this page and I think it is going to be about… because…

Are there any words you don't know?

Let's check: feathered

Who has a question about what we have read?

How do you think the scientists knew that the Gigantoraptor was young when it died?

Other Huge Birds

I am looking at this page and I think it is going to be about… because…

Other fossils of huge birds have been found. One was the Stirton's Thunderbird. It had a **massive** beak, thick neck and huge clawed feet.

After the dinosaurs died, large birds called Terror birds lived on. These birds had huge beaks too. Scientists think that they caught **prey** in their beaks. Then they used their beaks to **crush** the prey.

Terror birds also had enormous **skulls**. They had skulls the size of a horse's head.

Are there any words you don't know?

Who has a question about what we have read?

Let's check: skulls

What do you think might have been prey for Terror birds?

Big – Good or Not So Good?

I am looking at this page and I think it is going to be about... because...

These other birds were big, but the Gigantoraptor was even bigger.

Scientists think that it was easier for larger animals to get food. Larger animals could also fight off **predators** more easily.

However, being too big was also a problem. Big animals like the Gigantoraptor would have needed a lot of food to eat and a lot of space.

Are there any words you don't know?

Who has a question about what we have read?

Let's check: predators

What do you think might be a problem if there were too many Gigantoraptors?

What Next?

I am looking at this page and I think it is going to be about... because...

Although scientists know a lot about dinosaurs, there is still much to learn. Xu Xing said, "If you saw a mouse as big as a pig, you would be surprised." That is what it was like to find the Gigantoraptor. It was a huge surprise.

Scientists keep looking for animals that have never been seen before. Who knows what they might find next?

Are there any words you don't know?

Who has a question about what we have read?

Let's check: examines

Why do you think scientists keep looking for animals they have never seen before?

Xu Xing **examines** a newly discovered fossil.

Something to Think About or

An old discovery

Description:

A new discovery

Description:

Think about bird-like dinosaurs – the ones discovered a long time ago and the one discovered not long ago. Can you imagine one that might be discovered in the future? Talk about your ideas with a partner, or draw and write about them.

A future discovery (Imagine!)

Description:

Do You Need to Find an Answer?

You could go to . . .

Library

Expert

Internet

Do You Want to Find Out More?

You could look in books or on the internet. These key words could help you:

Gigantoraptor

Stirton's Thunderbird

Terror birds

Xu Xing

Word Help

Dictionary

daggers	short swords with sharp edges used as weapons
crush	to squash
examines	studies something carefully
feathered	covered with feathers
flees	runs away from something
fossil	a part of a plant or animal that has been in the ground for millions of years and has become hard like a rock
massive	very large and very solid
model	a copy of something usually made on a smaller scale
ostrich	a large African bird with two toes that can run very fast but cannot fly

predators	animals that hunt, kill or eat other animals to survive
prey	an animal or animals that are caught, killed and eaten by another animal for food
skulls	the bony framework inside heads
Tyrannasaurus rex	a large, meat-eating dinosaur with huge teeth
Velociraptors	small, meat-eating dinosaurs

Word Help

Thesaurus

caught	trapped
enormous	vast, mammoth, huge, gigantic, massive
massive	enormous, huge, gigantic
probably	likely
sharp	pointed, jagged
snapping	biting
surprise	astonish, amaze
tearing	ripping
uncovers	unearths, reveals

Location Help
Where Gigantoraptor Was Found

Index

beak 6, 10

claws 6–7, 10

feathers 6, 8

fossil 4–5, 6–7, 10, 15

ostrich 6, 9

predators 12

Stirton's Thunderbird 10–11

Terror birds 10–11

Tyrannosaurus rex 4

Xu Xing 4–5, 6–7, 14–15